"G" Is for Geography

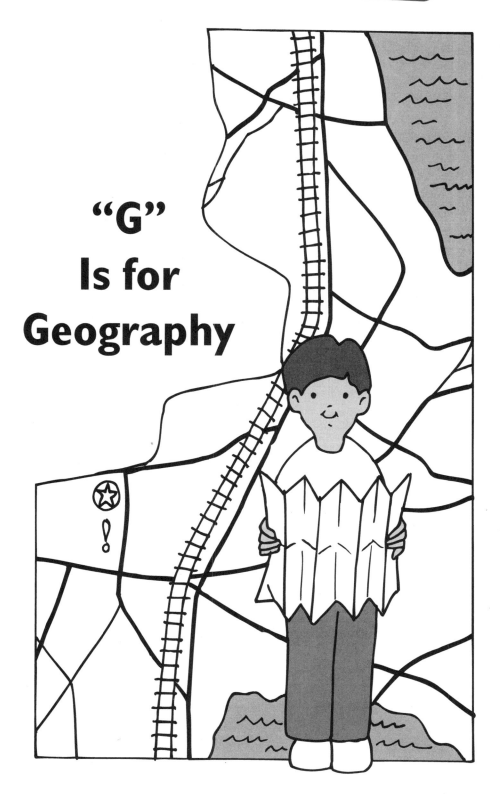

by Annalisa McMorrow
illustrated by Marilynn G. Barr

Dedicated to Ronald & Kirsten, our friends around the world.

Publisher: Roberta Suid
Design & Production: Alex Mendra
Cover Design: David Hale

Entire contents copyright © 2002 by
Monday Morning Books, Inc.
For a complete catalog, please write to the address below:

P.O. Box 1680
Palo Alto, CA 94302

E-mail us at: MMBooks@aol.com
Visit our Web site: www.mondaymorningbooks.com

ISBN 1-57612-153-4

Printed in the United States of America
987654321

Contents

Railroad

Airport

River

Mountain

Bay

Capital

Lake

Introduction

G Is For Geography is a month-long unit filled with informative and exciting cross-curriculum activities. Geography-related history, language, math, art, spelling, homework, and game activities are featured for each week. Songs are also included.

Use the "Geography Facts" (p. 6) to introduce the unit. This sheet features symbols used in geography. Then help children make their map-covered Geography Portfolios. They can use these to store all of their geography-related activities, or to take materials home to share with their families.

Patterns throughout the unit can serve many purposes. For instance, some will work for use as name tags, or desk or cubby labels. You can also enlarge patterns to use as bulletin board decorations.

The activities in G Is For Geography are intended for grades one through three. Each week focuses on a different national standard for geography study. Some lessons may easily be simplified for younger children. For instance, if children cannot write their own reports or stories, they can dictate them to the teacher or teacher's helper, record them on a tape recorder for an audio report, or draw pictures to represent the words.

Graphic organizers and helpful patterns accompany several activities. These forms help the children to stay focused on the topics that they are researching or learning about.

The unit ends with a final game that allows children to share the knowledge that they've learned over the four week unit. Once children have finished the game, give the students Geographer Diplomas (p. 64), to show that they have mastered the beginning concepts of geography.

To extend the *G Is for Geography* unit, look for geography-related books to store in your reading corner. These might include books in which the characters take a trip that could be followed on a map, such as *The Little House on the Prairie* by Laura Ingalls Wilder. Or the books might be about people or locations in different parts of the world.

Challenge children to be on the lookout for mentions of travel, maps, habitats, or ecosystems in books and magazines that they read on their own. You might be surprised at the map references that you or the children find. For instance, in the comic strip "Family Circle," a map is sometimes featured that shows the travels of the character Billy as he makes his way through the neighborhood.

The Web is also a good place to locate information, especially about foreign locations. Remember, Web sites change with frequency. Always check the sites yourself before sharing them with the students.

Below are several books to use to gather facts and pictures to share with the students.

Geography-related Books:

• *Geography Coloring Book* by Wynn Kapit (Addison-Wesley)
• *Geography Wizardry for Kids* by Margaret Kenda (Barrons Juveniles)
• *Homes Around the World* by Bobbie Kalman (Crabtree)
• *Homes Around the World* by Jenny Mumford (Raintree)
• *Houses and Homes* (Around the World Series) by Ann Morris (Mulberry Books)
• *Mapping the Skies* by Walter G. Oleksy (Watts Library)
• *Maps and Plans* (Geography for Fun) by Pam Robson (Copper Beech Books)
• *What Do We Know About Grasslands?* (Caring for Environments) by Brian J. Knapp (Peter Bedrick Books)

Geography Facts

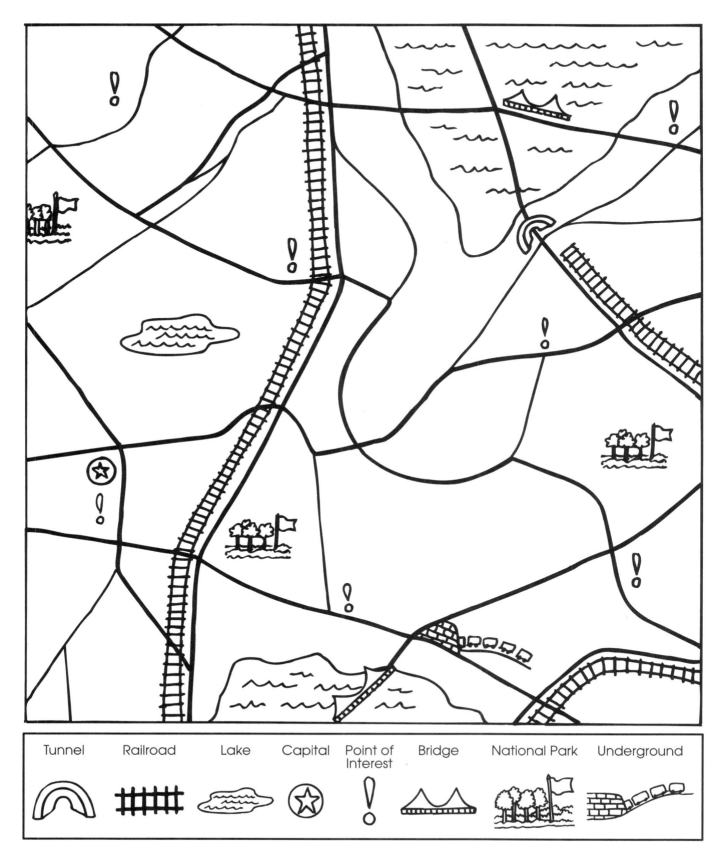

| Tunnel | Railroad | Lake | Capital | Point of Interest | Bridge | National Park | Underground |

G Is for Geography © 2002 Monday Morning Books

Geography Portfolio

Materials:
Portfolio Patterns (p. 8), scissors, crayons or markers, glue, hole punch, yarn, legal-sized folders or large sheets of heavy construction paper

Preparation:
Duplicate a copy of the Portfolio Patterns for each child.

Directions:
1. Demonstrate how to make a portfolio. If using legal-sized folders, punch holes along the two open sides. Cut two arm-length pieces of yarn and tie knots in one side of each. Thread the yarn through the holes and tie the free ends together to make a strap. If using construction paper, fold the paper in half to make a folder, and then continue as described above.
2. Give each child a sheet of patterns to color and cut out.
3. Have the children decorate their portfolios with crayons, markers, and the patterns.

Options:
• The children can add their own hand-drawn pictures, as well. Or they can cut out pictures from magazines to glue to their portfolios.
• Provide old maps for the children to use to decorate their portfolios. (Ask for donations from home.)
• Cover the portfolios with contact paper for added sturdiness. Reinforce the holes with hole reinforcers.

Portfolio Patterns

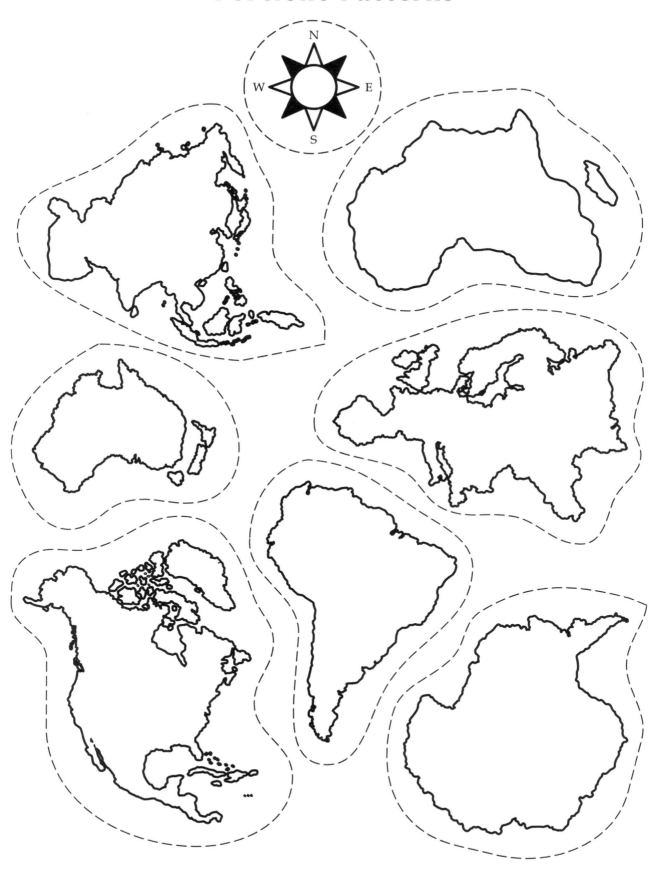

G Is for Geography © 2002 Monday Morning Books

Star-Studded Maps

Throughout history, travelers have looked to the stars to help chart their course. Familiar constellations are used as guides for directions. Children will have a chance to search for constellations in the night sky, just as travellers have for centuries.

Materials:
Map of the Stars (p. 10), star stickers (optional)

Preparation:
Duplicate a copy of the Map of the Stars for each child.

Directions:
1. Explain to the children that many different types of maps exist. There are globes, atlases, road maps, three-dimensional maps, story maps, and so on.
2. Give each child a Map of the Stars to observe. Children can add star stickers to the maps, if desired.
3. Have the children take the maps home. They should try to spot as many of the constellations shown as possible.

Options:
• The children can create their own maps of the constellations using crayons, markers, star stickers, or by hole punching the constellations from sheets of black paper.
• Bring in an assortment of maps to share with the children for use during step one of this activity.

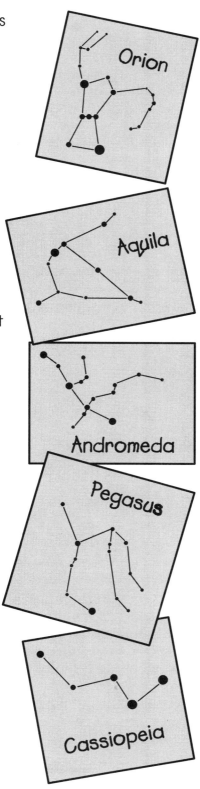

Map of the Stars

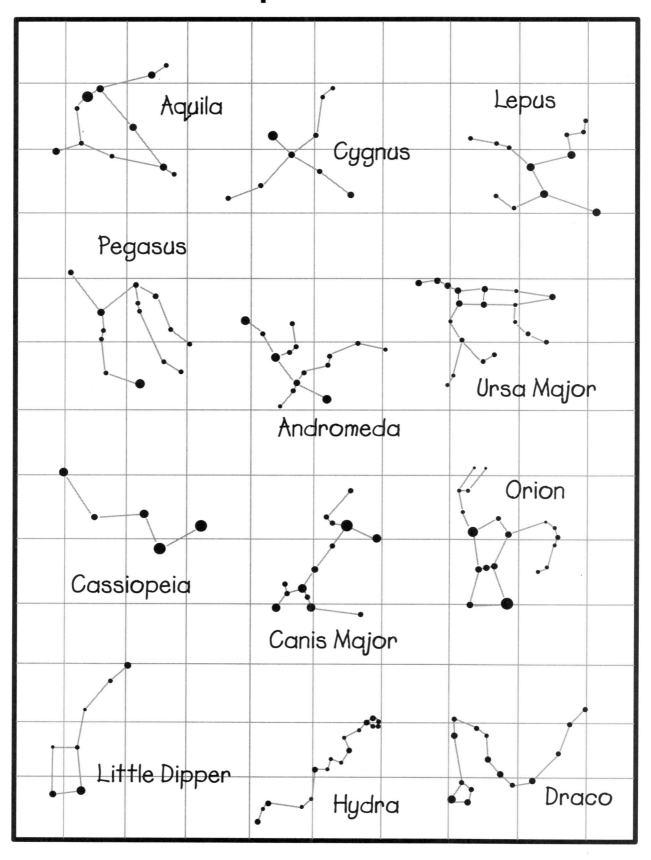

Mapping a Story

Choose a story with an interesting location to map. For instance, using the Harry Potter series, children might make a map of Harry's school, or of the region where Harry and his friends buy their schoolbooks, brooms, and so on.

Materials:
Large sheets of poster board, crayons or markers, children's books to map

Preparation:
Gather books ahead of time.

Directions:
1. Divide the children into small groups. Have each group choose a story to map. Explain that the children can make a map of a specific location or region. Or they can map a trip taken by the characters. (See the suggested list on this page.)
2. On the poster board, have the children work together to create maps of locations or routes traveled.
3. Invite each group to share their finished project with the rest of the students.

Options:
• Work together as a class to make a larger map.
• Let the children choose their own stories to map.

Stories to Map:
• The route traveled by the Ingalls in *The Little House on the Prairie* by Laura Ingalls Wilder.
• The route taken by Pongo and Missis in *The Hundred and One Dalmatians* by Dodie Smith.
• The journey through the chocolate factory in *Charlie and the Chocolate Factory* by Roald Dahl.
• The location in a folk tale or fable, such as "The Three Billy Goats Gruff," "Hansel and Gretel," or "Goldilocks."

How Many Houses?

This math activity can be used for different levels of mathematical study. For younger children, write a plus or minus on the hydrant of each equation. Write in a multiplication sign for older children.

Materials:
Mapping Math (p. 13), pencils, crayons or markers

Preparation:
1. Fill in the missing signs (+, -, or x), then duplicate the Mapping Math page. Make one for each child.
2. Make an answer key for self-checking, if desired.

Directions:
1. Give each child a copy of the Mapping Math.
2. Have the children do the problems. They count the houses on the first street, see whether they are doing an addition, subtraction, or multiplication problem, then look at the numeral after the hydrant. They draw the correct number of houses or the correct numeral on the final street.
3. Children can share their answers with the class. Or they can use the answer key for self-checking.

Options:
• For older children, pass out the Mapping Math pages without any symbols written in the hydrants. Let the children make their own problems to test their friends. They can add a +, -, or x and then write the answers on the back. Have the children trade papers.
• To make the problems more difficult, add more houses to the streets or write in larger numerals.

Mapping Math

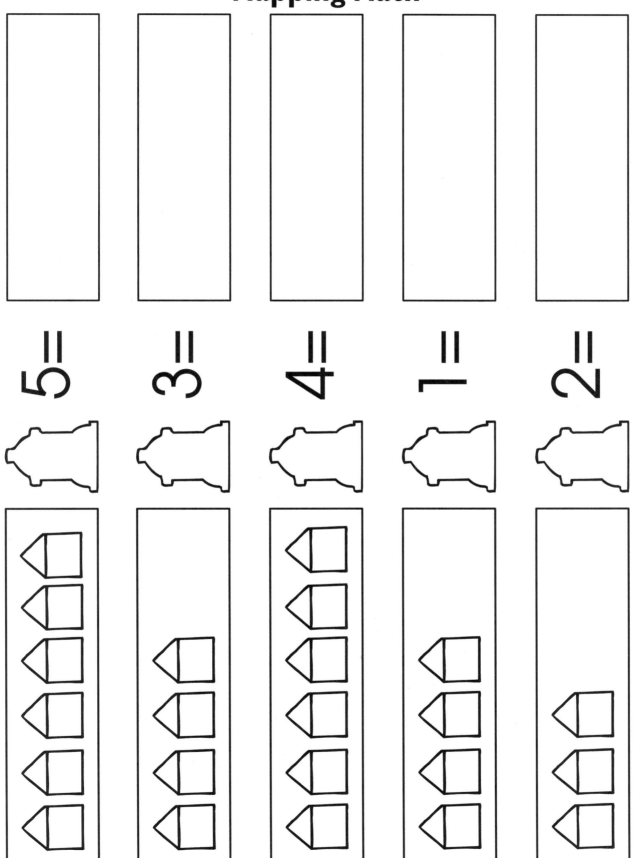

Spelling on a Map

Materials:
Map Symbols (p. 15), Map (p. 16), bag, construction paper, scissors, colored markers

Preparation:
1. Duplicate a copy of the spelling words for each child and one for teacher use.
2. Cut the words apart and color as desired.
3. Enlarge the map pattern and post on a bulletin board.

Directions:
1. Announce a date for a spelling "bee."
2. Divide the students into small groups. Have the children work together to learn the words. Let the children take the words home to study.
3. On the day of the spelling bee, put the spelling words in a bag. Pull one word from the bag at a time and have a child spell the word.
4. If the child spells the word correctly, he or she can post the word on the map. If not, another child tries to spell the word.
5. Continue until each child has a chance to spell one word and all of the symbols are posted on the map.

Option:
• Re-use words to let each child have a turn.

Map Symbols

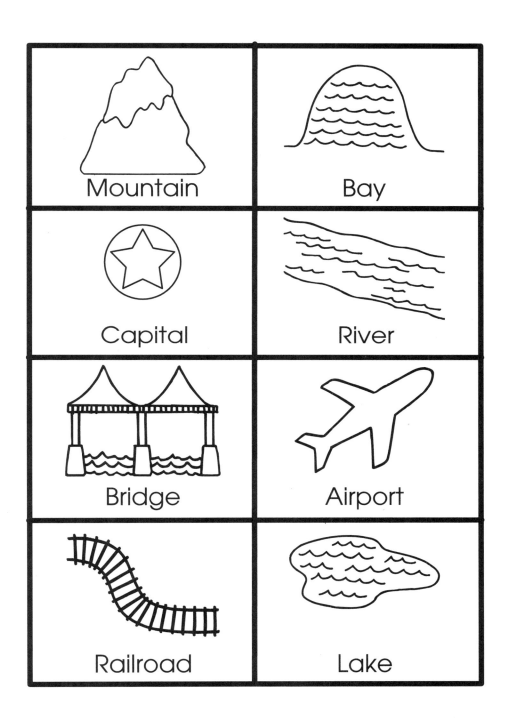

Mountain

Bay

Capital

River

Bridge

Airport

Railroad

Lake

Map

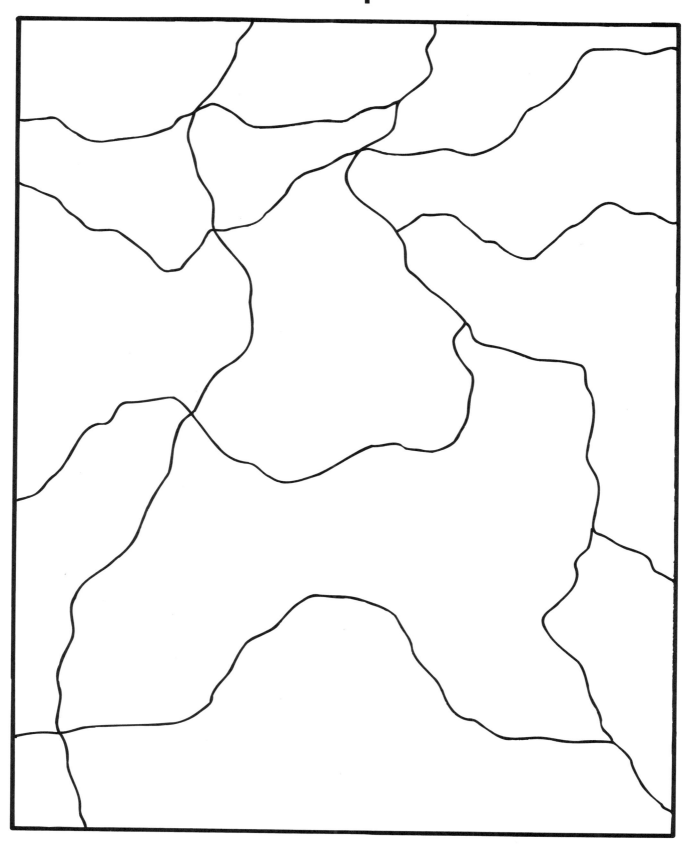

3-D Story Maps

You can make a large map as a class, or have the children work in the same small groups they did when mapping a story. They can now make a three-dimensional map of the drawing that they did before.

Materials:
Poster board, crayons or markers, construction paper, scissors, glue, cardboard boxes and tubes, milk cartons, modeling clay, tempera paint, shallow tins (for paint), paintbrushes, decorative items (sequins, glitter, buttons)

Preparation:
None

Directions:
1. Have the children work together in small groups to plan their map.
2. Children can add clay mountains, blue sequin rivers, cardboard tube trees, milk carton or cereal box houses and buildings, and so on. Encourage creativity!
3. Once the children have finished their three-dimensional map, they can make a symbol key referencing the different landmarks, mountains, waterways, roads, railroad crossings, or any other significant items.
4. Display the symbol keys with the three-dimensional maps in the room, and invite parents or other students to view the maps.

Option:
Provide additional toy items for children to add to their maps, such as cars, trucks, or plastic people.

Matching Map Symbols

This concentration game will help children master the meanings of different map symbols.

Materials:
Map Symbols (p. 15), crayons or markers, scissors, clear contact paper

Preparation:
1. For each game, make two copies of the patterns.
2. Color as desired, cover with clear contact paper for protection, and cut out.

Directions:
1. To play the game, the players turn all of the cards face down. Then they take turns flipping two cards over. If the pictures on the cards match, they keep both and try again. If the cards don't match, they turn them face down and another child takes a turn.
2. The children can take the concentration game home to play with their families.

Option:
Older children can practice spelling the names of the symbols as they turn over the cards.

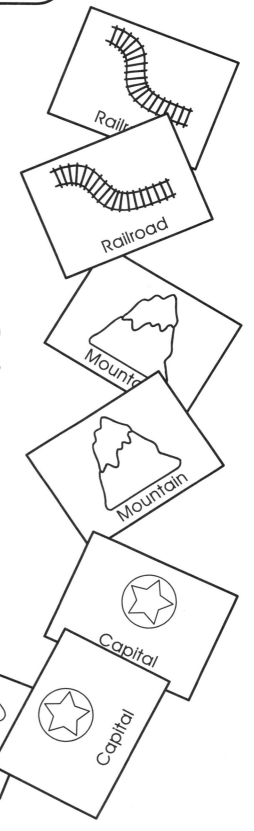

Map Songs

I Could Use a Map
(to the tune of "Home on the Range")

I'm lost, don't you know?
I don't know where to go.
Nothing looks like a place that I've been.
I look but don't see
Things familiar to me.
I'm helpless in the state that I'm in.

Maps lend you a hand.
They show where you are on the land.
Yes, a map would help me
Find where I want to be.
Oh, a map would show me where I stand.

A Map Is a Picture of Places
(to the tune of "My Bonnie Lies Over the Ocean")

A map is a picture of places.
It tells you what you want to know.
You follow a set course that traces,
Exactly where you want to go.

Seeing Signs

Materials:
Tallying Signs (p. 21), pens or pencils

Preparation:
Duplicate a copy of the Tallying Signs sheet for each child.

Directions:
1. Explain that the children will be tallying the number of different signs they see in their neighborhoods.
2. Give each child a Tallying Signs sheet to take home. Have them observe the number of different types of signs they see with specific directions—for instance, have them tally how many signs they see in their block, on their way home from school, or over a period of several days.
3. When the children bring back their filled-in sheets, use them in a class graph.

Option:
Take the children on a walk through the neighborhood to tally signs around the school.

G Is for Geography © 2002 Monday Morning Books

Tallying Signs

Name:

Date:

Put a check mark by each symbol every time you see one. If you see a sign that isn't on this sheet, draw a picture of it on the back.

Stop sign:

Stop light:

One way:

Railroad crossing:

Children crossing:

School zone:

Hospital:

Do Not Enter:

Our Turn-of-the-Century Town

In this activity, children will learn about what their town was like over 100 years ago! Consider inviting a member of the historical society to speak about the past.

Materials:
Poster board, crayons or markers, construction paper, scissors, glue, cardboard boxes and tubes, milk cartons, modeling clay, tempera paint, shallow tins (for paint), paintbrushes, decorative items (sequins, glitter, buttons)

Preparation:
Gather information about your town at the turn of the century. Your historical society or city hall should have information. You might find information on the Web. Or collect books about the turn of the century to share.

Directions:
1. Discuss differences in the way your town looked at the turn of the century. For instance, instead of a big highway, there might have been a field with cows. If possible, show pictures of your city long ago. If not, show pictures of cities from the same time.
2. Explain that the children will be working to make a replica of what their town might have looked like at the turn of the century. It doesn't have to be exact, but it should include items such as the school, city hall, libraries, post offices, and banks. If you have a photo, children can replicate what they see. The most important part may be what is *not* on the map—high-tech buildings, multiple-lane highways, multiplex movie theaters, and so on.

Option:
Ask the children to compare their town today with the town from the turn of the century. They can do so in a short written piece, or as oral reports.

Living Long Ago

After children have learned about life in the past, they can write a short story pretending that they are children at the turn of the century. Children can refer to the three-dimensional map of your town (p. 22) to get ideas.

Materials:
Paper, pens or pencils, encyclopedias and other resources

Preparation:
Gather resource materials.

Directions:
1. Explain that the children will be writing short stories from the point of view of a child who lived in your town at the turn of the century. Invite the children to close their eyes while you describe some of the experiences they might have had, living long ago. (See list on this page.)
2. Provide encyclopedias and other resource books for children to use to gather facts about the past. They can include these facts in their stories.
3. The children can write brief stories and illustrate them.
4. Have the children share their stories with the class.
5. Post the completed stories near the Turn-of-the-Century Town map.

Option:
Have the children dress up in period costumes to present their stories. The costumes can be very simple—boys would wear short pants (shorts would be fine), girls might tie on an apron as a pinafore or wear bonnets.

One-hundred Years Ago:
• Cars were very new and rare. Most people rode in carriages rather than cars.
• Television, video games, and hand-held play stations hadn't been invented. Children played different types of games, such as hide-and-seek.
• There was no e-mail. People wrote letters.
• People had milk and other dairy products delivered to their door each morning.

Stop Sign Math

This math activity can be used for different levels of mathematical study. For younger children, write a plus or minus in the center stop sign. Write in a multiplication sign for older children.

Materials:
Stop Sign Math (p. 25), pencils, crayons or markers

Preparation:
1. Fill in the missing signs (+, -, or x), then duplicate the Stop Sign Math page. Make one for each child.
2. Make an answer key for self-checking, if desired.

Directions:
1. Give each child a copy of the Stop Sign Math.
2. Have the children do the problems. They count the cars on the first street, look at the numeral, then see whether they are doing an addition, subtraction, or multiplication problem. They draw the correct numeral or number of cars on the final street.
3. Children can share their answers with the class. Or they can use the answer key for self-checking.

Options:
• For older children, pass out the Stop Sign Math pages without any symbols written in the stop signs. Let the children make their own problems to test their friends. They can add a +, -, or x and then write the answers on the back. Have the children trade papers.
• To make the problems more difficult, add more cars to the streets.

Stop Sign Math

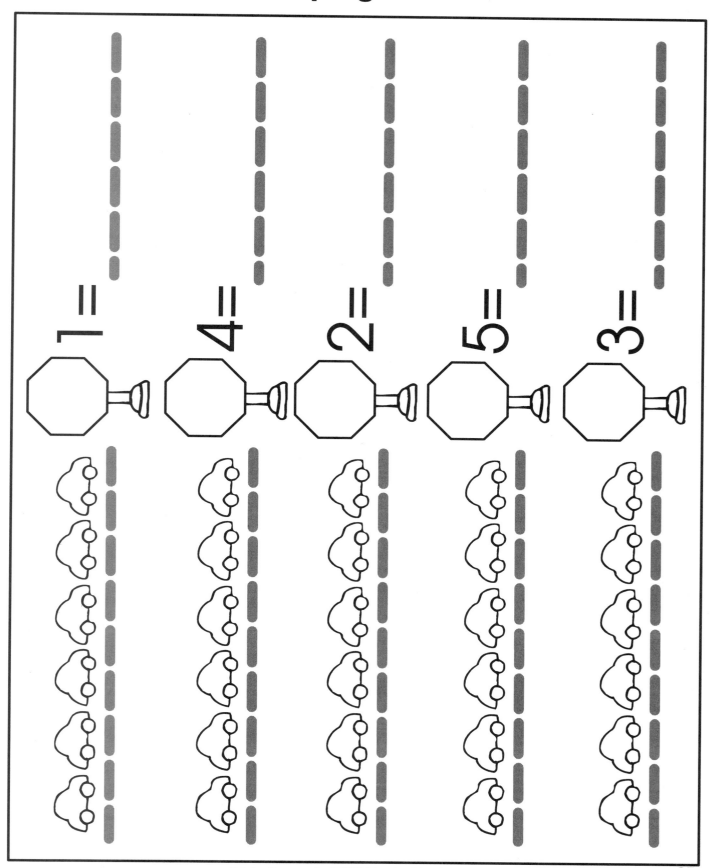

Signs Spelling Bee

Materials:
Signs (p. 27), scissors, crayons or markers, colored construction paper, tape

Preparation:
1. Duplicate a copy of the spelling word patterns for each child and one for teacher use.
2. Cut the spelling words apart and color as desired.
3. Create a bulletin board display that looks like a street using gray and black construction paper and crayons or markers.

Directions:
1. Announce a date for a spelling "bee."
2. Divide the students into small groups. Have the children work together to learn the words. Let the children take the spelling words home to study.
3. On the day of the spelling bee, put the words in a bag. Pull one from the bag at a time and have a child spell the word.
4. If the child spells the word correctly, he or she can post the word on the street display. If not, another child tries to spell the word.
5. Continue until each child has a chance to spell one word, and all of the words are posted.

Options:
• Use the blank Signs to make enough words for each child in the classroom to spell at least one. Or re-use words to let each child have a turn.
• White-out the given spelling words and write in other geography-related words.

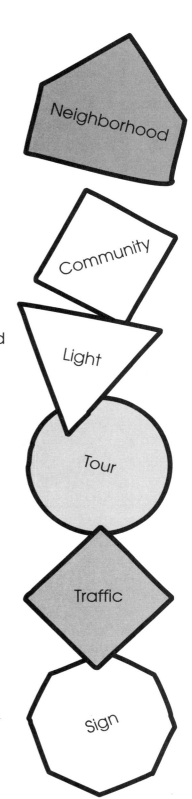

Signs

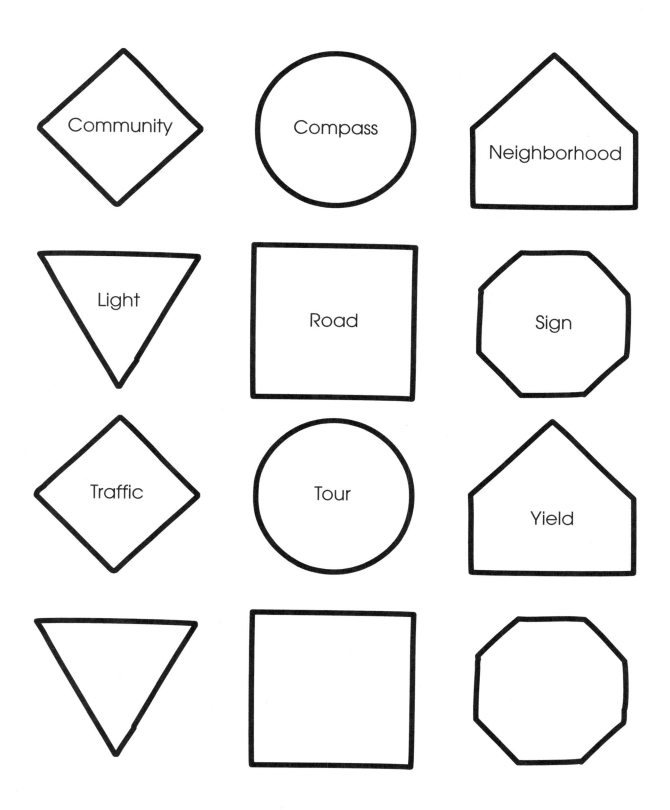

Community

Compass

Neighborhood

Light

Road

Sign

Traffic

Tour

Yield

Tourist Brochures

Children will create brochures that give information about their towns. Each brochure will explain features that the children most enjoy or appreciate.

Materials:
Brochure Pattern (p. 29), pens or pencils, crayons or markers

Preparation:
1. Duplicate a copy of the Brochure Pattern for each child.
2. Gather travel brochures for children to observe. (These are often available from services such as AAA.)

Directions:
1. Give each child a Brochure Pattern.
2. If possible, show the children travel or tourist brochures from other places.
3. Have the children fold the brochures into thirds. On the front, the children will write the name of their town and draw a map of something that they think makes their town special.
4. Inside the brochures, the children will write information about their town.
5. Post the brochures on a bulletin board where other classes can observe them.

Options:
• Have the children do research and include facts in their brochures, such as the population of your town, the number of libraries or schools, and the annual amount of rainfall or snow.
• The children can write tourist brochures for their turn-of-the-century town.

Brochure Pattern

Geography Jeopardy

This game is played like the Jeopardy game show on television. However, in this case the children choose whether answers are true or false.

Materials:
Quiz Questions (p. 31), scissors, index cards, pencils, resource books about geography (an atlas, an encyclopedia, an almanac)

Preparation:
None

Directions:
1. Explain the game. You will read a question. Children who think they know if the answer is true or false will raise their hands. Choose one child to answer.
2. Once the children understand the game, have each child create his or her own true/false question. The children should write the question on one side of an index card and the answer on the back. They can use information from this book, or from resource books about geography.
3. Gather all of the children's questions and continue with the quiz game. Or let the children quiz each other.

Option:
Create a point system where questions are given a certain number of points based on the level of difficulty. Have a Final Jeopardy run-off between the children with the most points.

Geography Jeopardy
1. One hundred years ago, most people drove cars.

Geography Jeopardy
4. A symbol key opens a door.

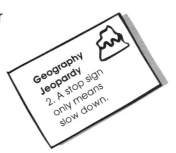

Geography Jeopardy
2. A stop sign only means slow down.

Geography Jeopardy
5. A globe is a flat picture of the world.

Geography Jeopardy
7. People have used the stars as maps.

Quiz Questions

1. One hundred years ago, most people drove cars.
False

2. A stop sign only means slow down.
False

3. A map can show mountains, rivers, and important landmarks.
True

4. A symbol key opens a door.
False

5. A globe is a flat picture of the world.
False

6. A book containing maps and symbol keys is called an atlas.
True

7. People have used the stars as maps.
True

Final Jeopardy Question:
On a map, different-sized type indicates the importance of a town or city.
True. Larger type means that a city is larger than a city with a name shown in smaller type.

My Town Songs

Neighborhoods and Locations
(to the tune of "Jingle Bells")

Neighborhoods and places in the vicinity.
Areas or districts, in the proximity.
Habitats and landmarks that you would like to see,
You'll find them on a map of your community!

A map will tell you things
That you would like to know.
Directions can be found
To where you would like to go.

Just spread the map out flat,
And follow all the signs.
The symbols and the keys,
Will help you make good time.

Oh, neighborhoods and places in the vicinity.
Areas or districts, in the proximity.
Habitats and landmarks, that you would like to see,
You'll find them on a map of your community!

Note: Some of the words in this song may be difficult for your children. Challenge the students to look up these words in the dictionary.

A Town...
(to the tune of "My Bonnie Lies Over the Ocean")

A town or a city or region,
A mountain, an ocean, a wood,
An area, suburb, or outskirts,
A district, or a neighborhood.

All of these places can be found by looking at maps,
At maps.
All of these places can be found by looking at maps!

Mapping My Room

Now that children are familiar with a variety of different types of maps, give them a chance to make maps of their bedrooms or houses.

Materials:
Paper, pens or pencils, crayons or markers

Preparation:
Create a map of your own home, classroom, or office to share with the children.

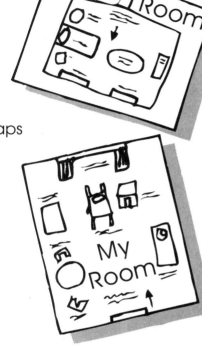

Directions:
1. Explain that the children will be making two-dimensional maps of their homes or bedrooms to share with their classmates.
2. Use your personal map to demonstrate the activity.
3. At home, have the children use plain paper and crayons or markers to draw maps of their rooms.
4. When the children bring the completed maps back to the classroom, give each child a chance to walk his or her classmates through the map.

Option:
Have children make maps of the homes or bedrooms of favorite storybook characters.

Family Map

Children will be interested in learning where their classmates' families originally came from.

Materials:
World Map (p. 35) or globe, crayons or markers, colored stick-on Post-its, encyclopedias, paper, pens or pencils

Preparation:
Duplicate and enlarge the World Map. Color as desired.

Directions:
1. Explain that the class will be working together to map where the children's different relatives originally came from.
Note: Have the children ask their parents for information about their ancestors.
2. Use Post-its to mark the different countries where children's families originally lived. Write each child's name on the appropriate Post-it.
3. Divide the class into small groups and have the children use encyclopedias to learn several facts about each location marked on your map.
4. Post the facts in a border around the family map.

Option:
Host international awareness days and invite children's relatives to speak about the different places where their families originally came from.

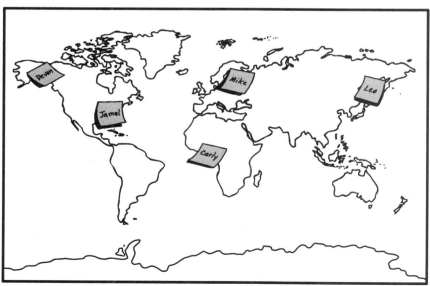

World Map

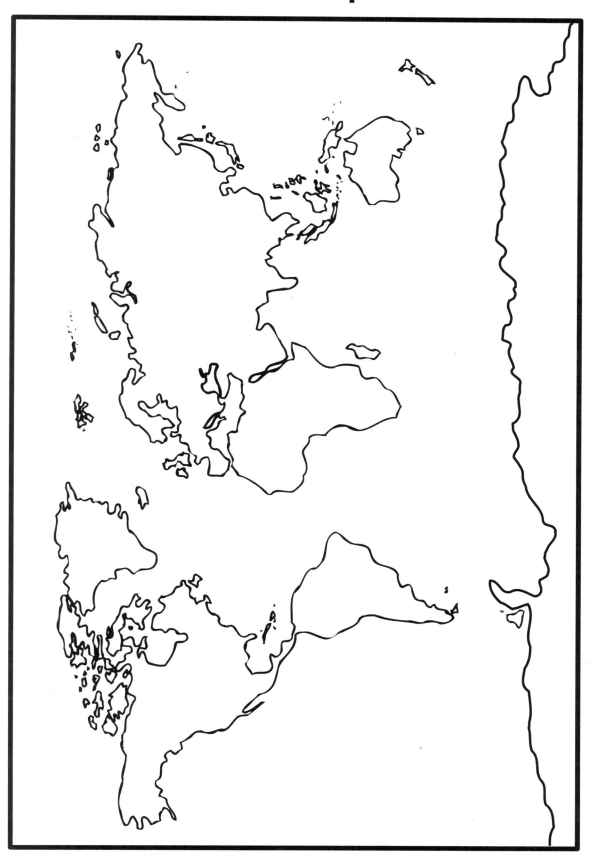

Making Pen Pals

Writing letters is one way to strengthen a child's language skills. Pen pals allow children to learn about regions around the world.

Materials:
Paper, pens or pencils

Preparation:
None

Directions:
1. Explain the concept of pen pals to the children. Pen pals from different countries exchange letters. They then learn about their new pal's environments.
2. If you are going to join a pen pal group, decide whether to write a letter as a class, or have the children write individual letters. If the children are each writing letters, give them prompts for what to write about—such as their town, their neighborhood, their houses, or their school.
3. On a map or globe, keep track of the different countries in which the pen pals live.

Option:
Children can either write to real pen pals, or they can write and answer letters from each other. To do this, children would pretend to be from different countries. They would exchange letters, research to answer questions, and then write responses.

Pen Pal Club:
• Children Just Like Me Pen Pal Club
This club aids UNICEF. For more information, write to the Make a Friend Pen Pal Club, DK Publishing, 95 Madison Avenue, New York, NY 10016

Shape Shifting

This activity focuses on mastering the concept of continents while teaching a simple geometry lesson.

Materials:
Large world map, paper, pens or pencils, chalkboard, chalk

Preparation:
None

Directions:
1. Show the children the world map.
2. Point out the seven different continents: Africa, Antarctica, Asia, Australia, Europe, North America, and South America.
3. Explain that the children will be drawing their own representations of the continents using only shapes.
4. Demonstrate this activity using chalk. Then let the children try to make their own world maps using circles, ovals, rectangles, squares, and triangles.
5. Have the children label the different continents. Then post the completed pictures on a bulletin board.

Option:
Provide shapes (such as jar lids or boxes) for children to trace to make their pictures.

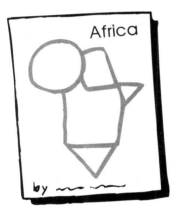

Dwellings Spelling

Materials:
Houses (p. 39), bag, construction paper, scissors, colored markers

Preparation:
1. Duplicate a copy of the Houses for each child and one for teacher use.
2. Cut one set of the Houses apart and color as desired.

Directions:
1. Announce a date for a spelling "bee."
2. Divide the students into small groups. Have the children work together to learn the words. Let the children take the words home to study.
3. On the day of the spelling bee, put the spelling patterns in a bag. Pull one pattern from the bag at a time and have a child spell the word.
4. If the child spells the word correctly, he or she can post the house pattern on the bulletin board. If not, another child tries to spell the word.
5. Continue until each child has a chance to spell one word, and all of the house patterns are posted on the board.

Option:
Use the blank houses to make enough words for each child in the classroom to spell at least one. Or re-use words to let each child have a turn.

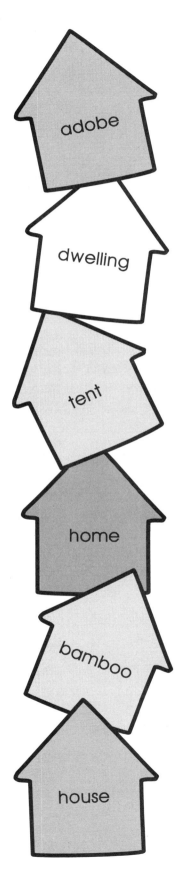

G Is for Geography © 2002 Monday Morning Books

Houses

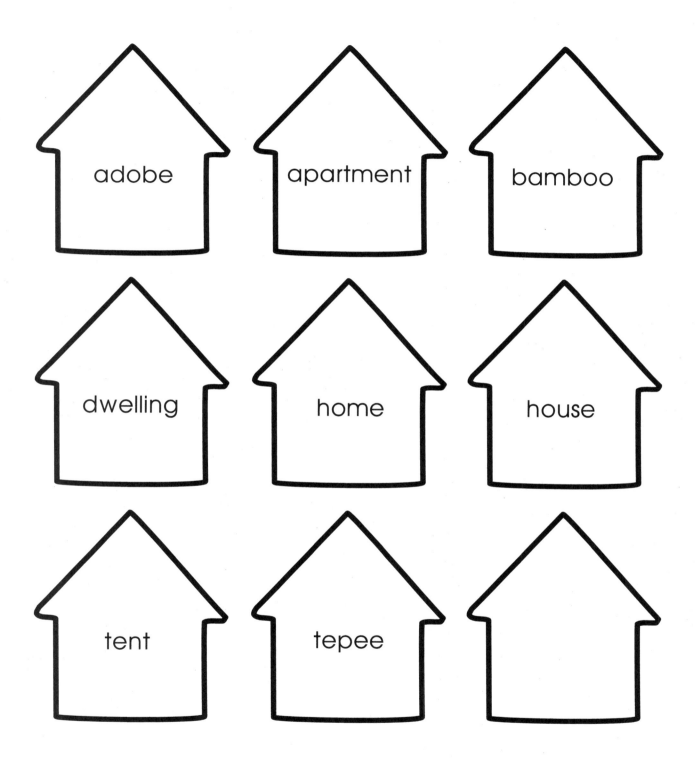

adobe

apartment

bamboo

dwelling

home

house

tent

tepee

Preparing a Passport

Children will see how many countries they can "visit" in this combined research and art activity.

Materials:
Passport (p. 41), Stamps (p. 42), manila folders (one per child), crayons or markers, pens or pencils, lined paper, tape or glue, books about children and families around the world

Preparation:
Duplicate a copy of the passport pattern and stamp patterns for each child.

Directions:
1. Give each child a passport pattern and a manila folder.
2. Have the children glue the patterns to the fronts of their folders. Inside the folders, they should tape or glue the lined paper.
3. Explain that the children will be collecting facts about families from around the world. For each fact that they write in their passport, they can glue a stamp to the back of the folder. Their goal is to collect as many facts (and stamps) as they can in a designated period of time.

Option:
Have each child do a report about a specific country. After listening to each report, the children would each add a stamp to their passports.

G Is for Geography © 2002 Monday Morning Books

Passport

Flag

Country

Name

Stamps

G Is for Geography © 2002 Monday Morning Books

Families Around the World

Around the world, families live together in different types of homes. This game lets children have a look at an assortment of houses in which people live.

Materials:
House Cards (p. 44), Fact Cards (p. 45), crayons or markers, scissors, envelopes (one per child)

Preparation:
Duplicate a copy of the cards for each child.

Directions:
1. Give each child a copy of the cards to color and cut apart.
2. Explain that these cards represent only a sampling of the many places that people live.
3. Have the children play a concentration game by turning all of the cards face down, then flipping over two at a time. The goal is to match the house cards with the fact cards.
4. When finished playing the game, the children can glue the cards to a large sheet of colored construction paper (with the pictures above the facts).

Book Links:
• *Children Just Like Me* by Barnabas & Anabel Kindersley (DK)
• *Wake Up, World!* by Beatrice Hollyer (Henry Holt)

Options:
• Challenge older children to research and find facts about the way people live around the world.
• Children can make books, putting the pictures and facts on facing pages. Children can also draw their own versions of the pictures and write or dictate their own text.

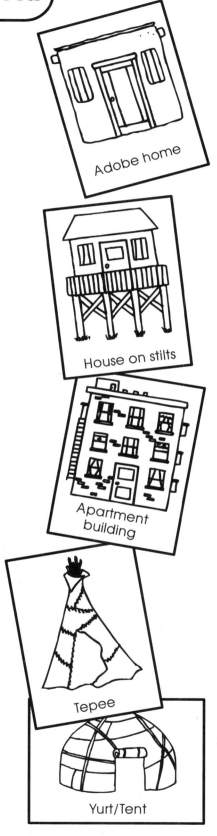

Adobe home

House on stilts

Apartment building

Tepee

Yurt/Tent

House Cards

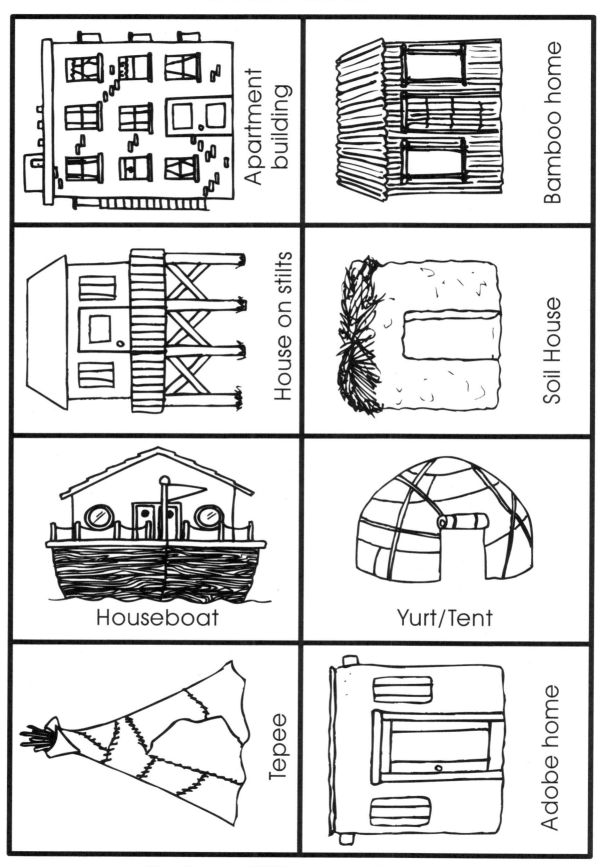

Apartment building

Bamboo home

House on stilts

Soil House

Houseboat

Yurt/Tent

Tepee

Adobe home

Fact Cards

 In New Mexico, many houses are made of adobe.

 In many parts of the world, people live in apartment buildings.

 In the Philippines, some houses are made of bamboo.

 In Indonesia, some houses are built on stilts.

 Houseboats are used by many different cultures.

 In southern Africa, some houses are made of soil and have grass roofs.

 A tepee, or wigwam, was an easy-to-move dwelling used by nomadic North American Indians.

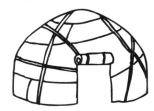 In Mongolia, nomads live in round tents called yurts.

Homes Around the World Song

A Family's Home
(to the tune of "My Bonny Lies Over the Ocean")

Some houses are made out of soil.
Some houses have roofs made of tin.
Some houses are tents in a circle.
That all relatives live within, within.

Homes are for families,
The families inside call them home, them home.
Homes are for families,
The families inside call them home.

A home is a place for a family.
Regardless of what it's made from.
Of soil, adobe, or bamboo,
The people inside call it home.

Homes are for families,
The families inside call them home, them home.
Homes are for families,
The families inside call them home.

G Is for Geography © 2002 Monday Morning Books

Discovering Directions

Prepare children for this take home activity by bringing a compass into the classroom. Let the children take turns locating north, south, east, and west.

Materials:
Compass

Preparation:
None

Directions:
1. The goal of this activity is to have the children pay attention to directions.
2. Challenge the students to find references to directions wherever they can. For instance, they may live on a street that includes the word North or South.
3. The children can look for references in newspapers, on town maps, in their neighborhoods, and so on. They can pay attention to where the sun sets (or rises), learning that the sun rises in the east and sets in the west.
4. Have the children share any references to directions that they discover.

Option
Take a class walking trip through the neighborhood, searching for references to directions.

North

East

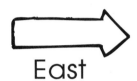

West

South

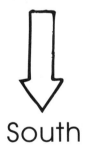

Exploring Ecosystems

Children will learn classifications of different ecosystems while researching our constantly changing environment.

Materials:
Eco-Organizer (p. 49)

Preparation:
Duplicate a copy of the Eco-Organizer for each child.

Directions:
1. Explain that environments often change over time. Sometimes, nature changes a place, such as by an earthquake or erosion. Other times, people help to change an environment. They might pipe water into a desert region to make farmlands. Or they might bulldoze hills or mountain regions to create flat lands where people can build houses.
2. As a class, research the changes that have taken place in your town's environment over a set period of years—perhaps 20, 50, or 100. You can use information from your city's historical society or city hall.
3. Give each child an Eco-Organizer to use to focus his or her research findings.
4. Have the children write reports on what they learn and share these reports with the class.

Option
Divide the children into groups and have the groups work on finding changes in different regions. They might research local farmlands, learn about a man-made lake or forest, explore logging conditions, learn about a region after an earthquake (such as Mount St. Helen's), and so on.

Eco-Organizer

Name: _____

Date: _____

The region I am studying is _____.

These are three ways that this area has changed over the past_____ years.

1. _____

   _____

2. _____

   _____

3. _____

   _____

Here is a drawing of what the area used to look like.

Here is a drawing of what the area looks like now:

Desert Trading Cards

Children will create desert trading cards featuring illustrations and facts about items found in a desert.

Materials:
Desert Cards (p. 51), desert resources, index cards cut in half, paper, pens or pencils, crayons or markers, scissors

Preparation:
1. Duplicate a copy of the cards for each child.
2. Gather desert-related books for children to use.

Directions:
1. Give each child a copy of the cards to color and cut apart.
2. Explain that the children will be making their own trading cards. Have the children choose a plant, animal, or other item found in the desert to research. (They can use the items on the desert cards, or come up with their own ideas.)
3. Have the children use books or the Web to find facts.
4. If the children are using the desert cards, they can simply write facts on the backs. If making their own cards, the children can draw a picture on one side of an index card and a fact on the back.
5. The children can trade cards, if they want to.

Options:
• Younger children can use the Desert Cards to play a game of concentration. Duplicate two copies of the cards for each game.
• Older children can add facts to their pictures.

cactus

camel

sand

oasis

tent

Desert Cards

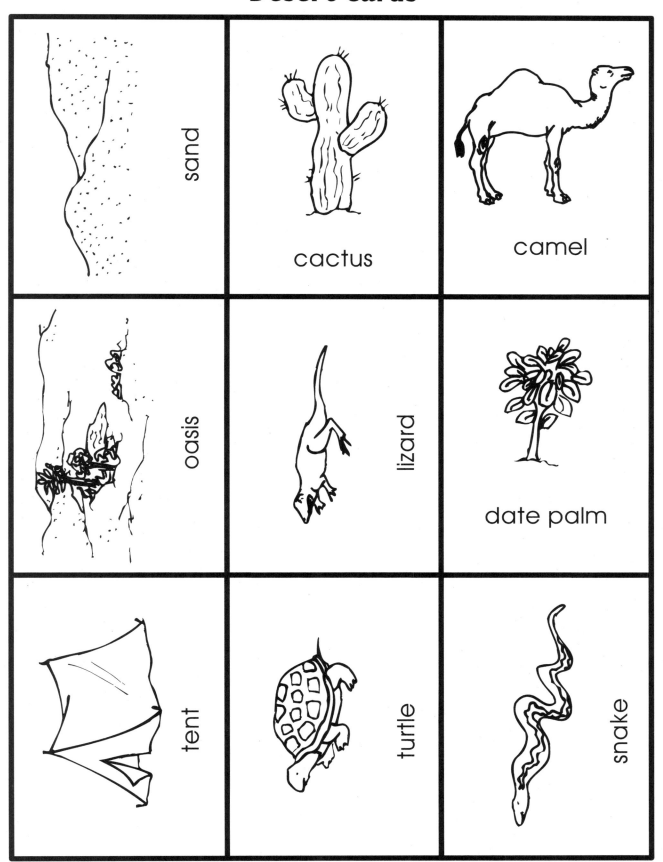

sand

cactus

camel

oasis

lizard

date palm

tent

turtle

snake

Mountain Math

Around the world, many different animals call the mountains their home. This math activity features pandas and can be used for different levels of mathematical study. For younger children, write a plus or minus in the box in each equation. Write in a multiplication sign for older children.

Materials:
How Many Pandas? (p. 53), pencils, crayons or markers

Preparation:
1. Fill in the missing signs (+, -, or x), then duplicate the math page. Make one for each child.
2. Make an answer key for self-checking, if desired.

Directions:
1. Give each child a copy of the math page.
2. Have the children do the problems. They count the pandas, see whether they are doing an addition, subtraction, or multiplication problem, then look at the numeral. They draw the correct number of pandas or write the correct numeral after the equals sign.
3. Children can share their answers with the class. Or they can use the answer key for self-checking.

Options:
• For older children, pass out the math pages without any symbols written in the boxes. Let the children make their own problems to test their friends. They can add a +, -, or x and then write the answers on the back. Have the children trade papers.
• To make the problems more difficult, add more pandas.

How Many Pandas?

☐ 3 =

☐ 1 =

☐ 5 =

☐ 2 =

☐ 4 =

Eco-Spelling

This activity will allow children to participate in creating a large, cooperative mural to feature the spelling patterns.

Materials:
Spelling Patterns (p. 55), bag, construction paper, scissors, colored markers, butcher paper, tempera paint, shallow tins (for paint), paintbrushes

Preparation:
1. Duplicate a copy of the patterns for each child and one for teacher use.
2. Cut one set of the patterns apart and color as desired.

Directions:
1. Announce a date for a spelling "bee."
2. Divide the students into small groups. Have the children work together to learn the words. Let the children take the words home to study.
3. Have the class create a class mural of different habitats. The children should be sure to make a representation of each ecosystem on the word list. Post the completed mural.
4. On the day of the spelling bee, put the words in a bag. Pull one word from the bag at a time and have a child spell the word.
5. If the child spells the word correctly, he or she can post the word on the correct part of the mural. If not, another child tries to spell the word.
6. Continue until each child has a chance to spell one word.

Option:
White-out the words on the patterns and write in other spelling words, such as animals that can be found in the different environments, or words such as "habitat," "environment," and "ecology."

G Is for Geography © 2002 Monday Morning Books

Spelling Patterns

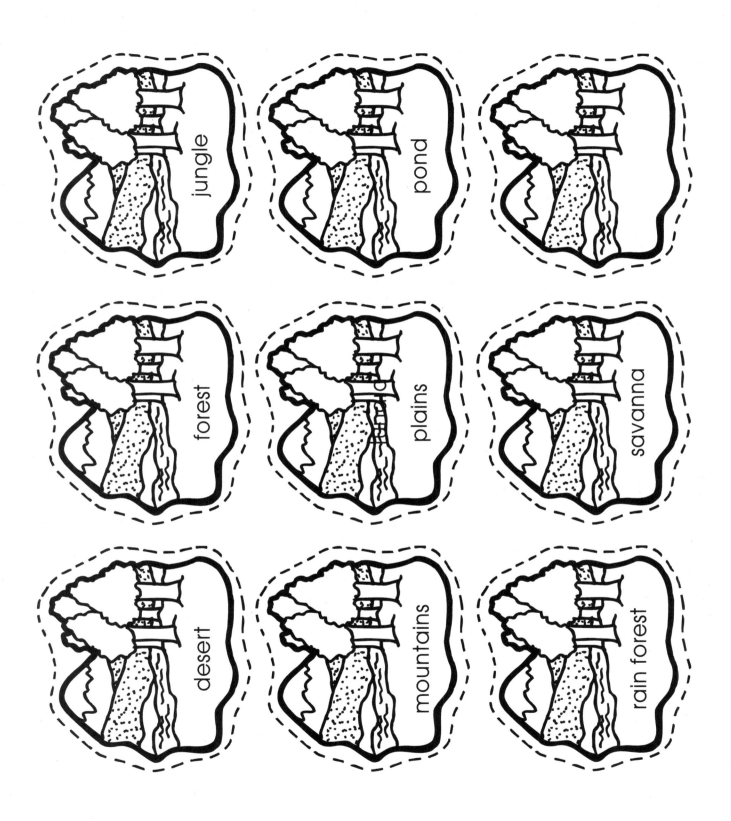

Matching the Ecosystems

Children will work to match animals with their habitats in this more advanced version of Concentration.

Materials:
Animal Patterns (p. 57), Habitat Patterns (p. 58), crayons or markers, scissors, clear contact paper

Preparation:
1. Duplicate one copy of each set of patterns for each game.
2. Color as desired, cover with clear contact paper, and cut apart.

Directions:
1. Demonstrate how to play the game. Players turn all of the cards face down. Then they take turns flipping two cards over. If the animal picture goes with the habitat picture, they keep both and try again. If the cards don't match, they turn them face down and another child takes a turn.
2. The children can take the concentration game home to play with their families.

Option:
Older children can make their own game pieces.

G Is for Geography © 2002 Monday Morning Books

Animal Patterns

Mountain goat

Black bear

Penguin

Koala

Chimpanzee

Lion

Habitat Patterns

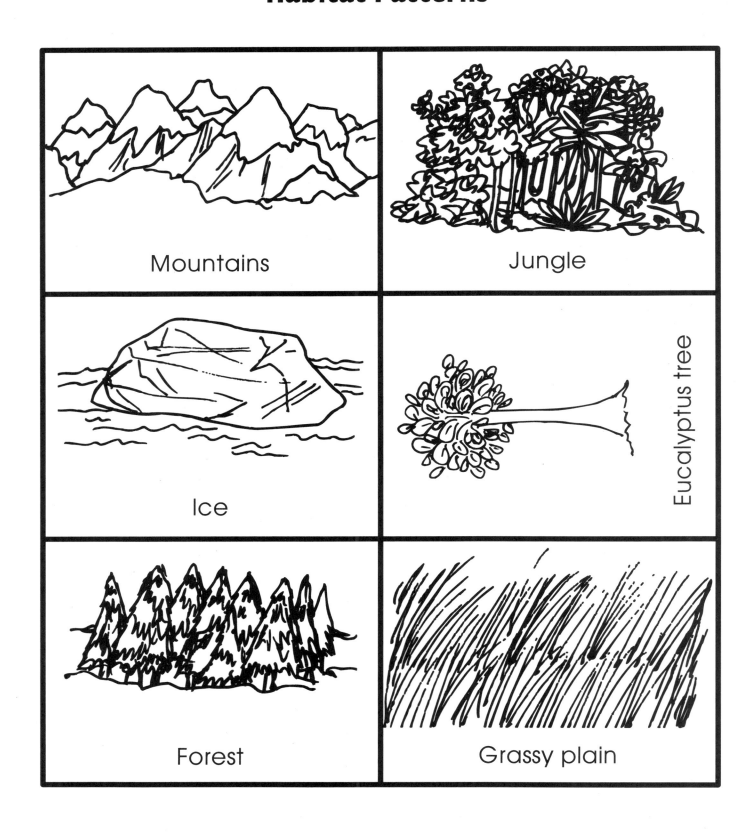

Mountains

Jungle

Ice

Eucalyptus tree

Forest

Grassy plain

Who Wants to be a Geographer?

Children will challenge each other with multiple-choice questions to share what they know about geography. Explain the term "geographer" ahead of time.

Materials:
Quiz Questions (p. 60), scissors, index cards, pencils, resource books about geography

Preparation:
None

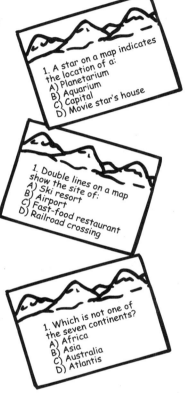

Directions:
1. Explain the game. You will read off a question and four possible answers. Children who think they know the answer will raise their hands. Choose one to answer. If he or she is correct, let this child read the next question. If not, keep going until a child answers correctly.
2. Once the children understand the game, have each child create his or her own question with four possible answers. The children should write the question and answers on one side of an index card and the correct answer on the back. They can use information from this book, or from resource books. Be sure to explain that three of the answers should be incorrect and only one will be correct.
3. Gather all of the children's questions and continue with the quiz game. Or let the children quiz each other.

Options:
• Let the children have a chance to remove two incorrect answers from the list.
• Allow children to confer with a friend about the correct answer.

Quiz Questions

1. A star on a map indicates the location of a:
A) Planetarium
B) Aquarium
C) Capital
D) Movie star's house
Answer: C

2. Double lines on a map show the site of a:
A) Ski resort
B) Airport
C) Fast-food restaurant
D) Railroad crossing
Answer: D

3. Children around the world live in different houses.
Which is not a type of dwelling?
A) Yurt
B) Hammock
C) Hut
D) Igloo
Answer: B

4. Which is not one of the seven continents?
A) Africa
B) Asia
C) Australia
D) Atlantis
Answer: D

5. Which is not a type of ecosystem?
A) Tundra
B) Savanna
C) Susannah
D) Desert
Answer: C

 G Is for Geography © 2002 Monday Morning Books

Eco-Songs

Oh, Savanna
(to the tune of "Oh Susannah")

A lion lives in grasses that are gold just like its mane.
It hunts and eats and sleeps all days in grasses and in plains.
Oh, savanna,
Tall grasses are for me.
You can find me sleeping in a veld that looks like a prairie.

In a Desert
(to the tune of "On Top of Old Smokey")

In a desert, on a mountain,
In the tundra, white with snow,
In a forest, on a prairie,
You can see the plant life grow.

Different plants and different creatures
Live and thrive across the land,
On a veld, or a savanna,
In a field or the grasslands.

Eco-Books

Children will put together little books about the different flora and fauna found in their local ecosystem.

Materials:
Book Patterns (p. 63), crayons or markers, scissors, stapler, construction paper

Preparation:
1. Duplicate a copy of the Book Patterns for each child.
2. Cut the construction paper to fit the book pages. Make two sheets per child.

Directions:
1. Give each child a copy of the Book Patterns to cut apart.
2. Help the children assemble their books. They can create front and back covers from colored construction paper.
3. Have the children take their books home. They should observe the different plant and animal life found in their neighborhoods. Have them draw pictures to represent the birds, plants, and animals that they see.
4. Children should record the information about the weather and seasons on the final page of the book.
5. When the children bring their books into the classroom, they can share their findings.

Option:
Children can do additional research to learn the scientific classifications for your environment. For instance, they can learn whether they live near a desert region, plains, forests, and so on. Often several types of ecosystems will be present.

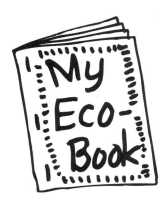

Book Patterns

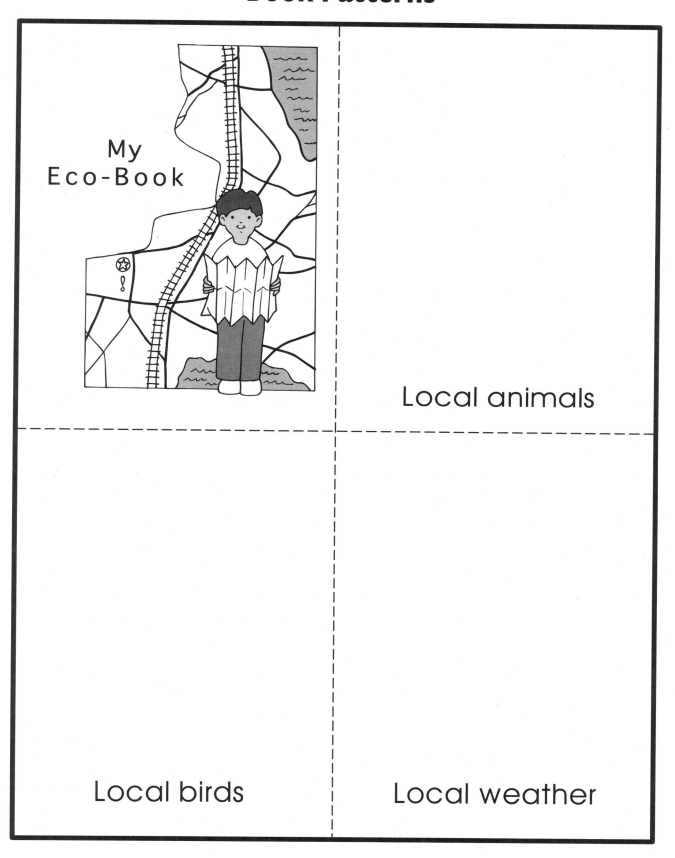

My
Eco-Book

Local animals

Local birds

Local weather

Name

HAS MASTERED

THE CONCEPT OF **GEOGRAPHY**

AND IS AN HONORARY GEOGRAPHER

HONORARY GEOGRAPHER